D0117581

Silent Storytellers

OF TOTEM BIGHT STATE HISTORICAL PARK

By Tricia Brown

Alaska Geographic Association
Anchorage, Alaska

The author offers deep appreciation to the elders for the invaluable lessons that they impart. And gratitude to those who helped bring this book about: Mary Kowalczyk, Totem Bight State Historical Park; Priscilla Schulte, Ph.D.; Nathan Jackson; Israel Shotridge; Lee Wallace; Lisa Oakley; Jill Brubaker; Chris Byrd; Debbie Whitecar; and JoAnne George.

Author: Tricia Brown
Photography: © B&C Alexander/Arcticphoto, p. 63; © Michelle Bates, p. 62; © Patrick J. Endres/AlaskaPhotoGraphics.com, p. 60; © Loyd Heath, cover, pgs. 18-19, 30-31, 34, 53, 54, 55, 56, 59, 61, back cover left; © John Hyde, p. 63; © Mary Kowalczyk, p 10; © 2009 Clark James Mishler/AlaskaStock.com, p 3; © Ron Niebrugge/wildnatureimages.com, pgs. iv, 22, 24, 26, 28, 32, 36, 38, 40, 42, 44, 46, 48, 50, 52, 57, back cover, center & right.
Historical Images: p. 1, CCC carvers, 1939, photo by Otto C. Schallerer, University of Washington Libraries, Special Collections, NA 3854; p. 2, left, Kasaan, ca. 1913, photo by John E. Thwaites, University of Washington Libraries, Special Collections, NA 3555; p. 2, right, Haida Indians in ceremonial dress at Klinkwan, ca. 1900, Alaska State Library, Winter and Pond, ASL_P87_0315; p. 7, right, Tlingit carver Charles Brown, photo by C. M. Archbold, University of Washington Libraries, Special Collections, NA 3636; pgs. 5-9, Foreman C. R. Snow's logbook courtesy of Alaska State Parks.
Legends reprinted from: Swanton, John R, *Tlingit Myths and Texts* (Washington, D.C.: U.S. Bureau of American Ethnology, Bulletin 39, 1909); Keithahn, Edward L., *Monuments in Cedar* (Seattle: Superior Publishing Co., [1963, c1945]); Garfield, Viola E. and Linn A. Forest, *The Wolf and the Raven: Totem Poles of Southeastern Alaska* (Seattle and London: University of Washington Press, [1986, c1961]); Serrill, Ward, Esther Shea, and Priscilla Schulte, *The Bear Stands Up: A Biography of Tlingit Tradition Bearer Esther Shea* (Ketchikan: University of Alaska Southeast, 1994)
Pole Illustrations: JoAnne George
Art Direction: Chris Byrd
Graphic Designer: Debbie Whitecar
Editor: Jill Brubaker
Project Manager: Lisa Oakley
Agency Coordinator: Mary Kowalczyk, Totem Bight State Historical Park

ISBN: 978-0-930931-97-1

© 2009 Alaska Geographic Association. All rights reserved.

810 East Ninth Avenue
Anchorage, AK 99501
www.alaskageographic.org

Alaska Geographic is the official nonprofit publisher, educator, and supporter of Alaska's parks, forests, and refuges. Connecting people to Alaska's magnificent wildlands is at the core of our mission. A portion of every book sale directly supports educational and interpretive programs at Alaska's public lands. Learn more and become a supporting member at www.alaskageographic.org

Library of Congress Cataloging-in-Publication Data

Brown, Tricia.
Silent Storytellers of Totem Bight State Historical Park / by Tricia Brown.
p. cm.
Includes bibliographical references and index.
ISBN 978-0-930931-97-1 (alk. paper)
1. Totem poles--Alaska--Totem Bight State Historical Park--History. 2. Totem Bight State Historical Park (Alaska) 3. Tlingit sculpture. 4. Haida sculpture. 5. Civilian Conservation Corps (U.S.)--Alaska--History. I. Title.

E98.T65B75 2009
979.8'2--dc22
2009015055

Printed in China on recycled paper.

Silent Storytellers

INTRODUCTION   1

MAP OF SOUTHEAST ALASKA   4

HISTORY OF TOTEM BIGHT   5

INTERPRETING THE SILENT STORYTELLERS   11

MAP OF TOTEM BIGHT   20

TOTEM POLES AND CLAN HOUSE   21

LEGENDS AND STORIES   52

A LIVING HERITAGE   61

TO LEARN MORE   64

Traditional Cultures and a Changing World

Long ago the Haida did not know how to carve,
and Master Carver came and taught them . . .

— The story of Master Carver as told by John Wallace

For centuries, the islands and cool, misty rainforests of Southeast Alaska have been home to the Tlingit Indians. Mountains, rivers, forest, and sea made up the boundaries of their world, yet they openly traded with other Native people beyond the passes and on distant shores. In recent centuries, chiefs in the southernmost Panhandle allowed neighboring tribes, the Haida and Tsimshian, to settle on Tlingit islands. Each group possessed its own unique ancestry, oral history, and legends, yet the three shared much in common.

Society here was highly developed when the American colonies were just declaring their independence from England. Along the coast, the first people hunted and fished, and fashioned clothing and tools from skins, bone, wood, and stone. They dwelt in homes of hewn wooden planks and traveled waterways in enormous dugout canoes. Storytellers, carvers, dancers, and drummers celebrated kinship and retold tales of their beginnings and historical adventures.

Among the coastal Indians, cultural memory was recorded in massive red cedars that were transformed in the hands of expert carvers. Extended family shared an expansive single-room house supported by carved upright logs called "house posts" that illustrated an important story belonging to that clan. Just outside, crests on soaring poles declared clan ownership. Other totem poles spoke of great events, or marked the grave of a great leader, or reminded others of an unpaid debt.

Then and now, central to the identity of each person was knowledge of belonging. In a complex social structure that

1

RIGHT: *Tlingit carvers working on a pole at Saxman in 1939.*

LEFT: *Haida totem poles and houses, Kasaan, Alaska, ca. 1913.*
BELOW: *Haida Indians in ceremonial dress outside Dogfish house at Klinkwan, ca. 1900.*

reached back before memory, every man, woman, and child belonged to a house group represented by a crest from nature, often a bird, fish, or animal, such as Killer Whale, Brown Bear, Frog, Thunderbird, Dogfish, among many. A clan was comprised of several house groups, and its members were like extended family with shared resources and history. The clan's ceremonial ways—stories, legends, dances, songs, honoring and remembering each other at potlatch celebrations—were passed from elders to youngsters, along with the practical knowledge of subsistence living.

Each clan was part of a specific tribe, the next level in the social order. Within each Tlingit and Haida tribe, children were born into one of two "moieties"—either Raven or Eagle/Wolf—in a matrilineal lineage. So if a mother was a Raven, her child was born a Raven. The social structure existed in villages throughout the vast region that's now known as the Alaska Panhandle. Each person could trace his or her ancestry through matrilineal family, house group, clan, tribe, and moiety.

The Tsimshian organization of tribes, or bands, was some-what different at the moiety level. Band members belonged instead to one of four "phratries"—Raven/Frog, Eagle, Wolf, or Killer Whale/Bear/Fireweed.

The divisions offered more than just identifying labels. Strict customs affected every area of life from birth to marriage to death. They demanded or prohibited who married whom and which clan performed certain duties, such as building a clan house, preparing the dead, or hosting a potlatch. The potlatch was an elaborate, multiday event—with feasting, dancing, singing, storytelling, and ceremonial gift-giving—that was given on great occasions, such as building a clan house, raising a totem pole, or remembering a death. If the occasion honored the Ravens, the Eagle/Wolf people hosted the potlatch, and vice versa, opposite clans respecting each other through reciprocal acts. Ownership of legends, stories, and songs dictated who could rightfully repeat them at a potlatch, and who was entitled to inherit those rights.

All three cultures followed the convention of matrilineal descent. If a Tlingit or Haida man were a Raven, he was required to marry across the moiety line and choose an Eagle/Wolf. In Tsimshian marriages, Eagle and Raven people could choose a spouse from the opposite phraties of Wolf and Bear. And while a father provided for his family, a boy's cultural education fell to his maternal uncle, whose clan matched his own. In earlier times, a boy even went to live with his uncle for training. While a physical move is no longer typical, the uncles still teach the history and traditions of their clan to the young.

Contemporary Tlingit, Haida, and Tsimshian people live in modern, single-family homes and take advantage of all the conveniences any other American does. But what remains unchanged in their cultures bears more importance than what has changed. In two hundred years, the people have adapted to various invasions of foreigners who, despite firepower, economic pressure, and force of government, were unable to strip away what is most critical: knowledge of self, and the manifold ways that knowledge is conveyed. Impermanent as they are, the totem poles themselves bear silent witness to endurance.

ABOVE: *Contemporary Tlingit children in traditional dress.*

CANADA

N

JUNEAU

CHICHAGOF
ISLAND

ADMIRALTY
ISLAND

BARANOF
ISLAND

SITKA

KAKE

KUIU
ISLAND

KUPREANOF
ISLAND

PETERSBURG

WRANGELL

S
O
U
T
H
E
A
S
T

PRINCE
OF WALES
ISLAND

TOTEM BIGHT STATE
HISTORICAL PARK

KETCHIKAN
SAXMAN

HYDABURG

ANNETTE
ISLAND

History of Totem Bight

We did not inherit this land from our ancestors;
we borrow it from our children.

— Haida Indian saying

In rare eighteenth-century images, masterfully carved totem poles tower above clan houses at villages like Klinkwan, Old Kasaan, Cape Fox, Sukkwan, Old Tongass, Kake, and Tuxekan. Each was once a thriving Native community that dwindled as families moved to larger towns for jobs and schooling. The old poles and clan houses remained, decaying with the decades. In the early 1900s, government officials and missionaries discouraged or outright barred Alaska Natives from their cultural practices, such as gathering for traditional feasts, singing, dancing, and speaking their first language. Carving itself came close to extinction.

The disintegration of old poles was not unusual in the eyes of the people. The process was as old as time. And yet, in the now uninhabited villages, no new totems would be raised to replace them. A few prominent individuals and organizations began sounding the alarm, driving totem salvage and restoration efforts.

Today's Totem Bight State Historical Park is the result of one such effort, a Civilian Conservation Corps (CCC) project that was launched in 1938. The CCC was created in 1933 when President Franklin D. Roosevelt signed the Emergency Works Progress Bill. Alaska Natives were juggling a subsistence lifestyle and a cash economy, with few available jobs, so a 1937 federal policy mandated that 50 percent of the CCC enrollees in Alaska must be Native. Workers would receive $1 a day, with a $25 monthly allotment sent to their

RIGHT: *Foreman C.R. Snow meticulously entered details in a logbook documenting the building of the Clan House at Totem Bight.*
LEFT: *Map of Southeast Alaska.*

South Corner Post nears completion

Jan. 27, 1941

families. All over the country, architects, artisans, and laborers were building public projects, laying in roads and recreational trails, and beautifying outdoor spaces. In the far north, Regional Forester B. Frank Heintzleman administered the totem pole restoration efforts as well as other CCC-Alaska Region projects as diverse as graveyard rehabilitation, wolf trapping, and airfield construction.

"Since most of these totem poles were in deserted Native villages inaccessible to regular steamer routes, the Forest Service desired to locate them more centrally where visitors to Alaska might enjoy these carved memorials," wrote Viola E. Garfield and Linn A. Forrest in their 1948 book, *The Wolf and the Raven.*

The move to salvage, replicate, or restore Alaska totem poles involved masterful coordination and cooperation among federal agencies, clans whose ancestors carved the old poles, field workers, and contemporary Native carvers working with apprentice teams.

Originally referred to as "Primitive Indian Village," and later as "Mud Bight Village," the Totem Bight project was spearheaded by two Forest Service men, project manager Linn A. Forrest and C. R. Snow, the on-site engineer and supervisor. They worked as a team with Tlingit lead carver, Charles Brown, and Haida head carver, John Wallace. The plan was to create a full-scale model village with plank houses, smokehouses, and totem poles representing both the Tlingit and Haida cultures.

After careful consideration, site selection was finalized. A traditional Tlingit campsite between lush forest and the ocean, it lay on the west side of Revillagigedo Island, with a gravel beach and salmon stream nearby. From the water, tourists on passenger ships or ferries could view the model village and soaring totems against a forested background. In a practical sense, the project would simultaneously inform visitors about the region's first people while supporting the carving tradition, as elders were employed to teach and supervise carving teams.

Besides Mud Bight Village, other totem parks were envisioned in the broad plan, including collections at New Kasaan, Saxman, Hydaburg, Klawock, Wrangell, and Sitka. Individual poles would be raised in the larger communities as well. The CCC carvers and their apprentices could count on steady employment for years and reconnect with the carvers in their ancestry.

"Even though the carvers knew they were doing this for tourism, they still did it for their own reasons," said Alaskan anthropologist Priscilla Schulte. "They knew this wasn't how they carved poles in the past, but it would perpetuate the art."

In 1938, Charles Brown was a full-time boat builder devoted to resurrecting totem carving. He saw the work as "the way for the uncles to teach the nephews," said Schulte, an adopted member of the Tlingit Bear Clan. Working with Brown was Haida elder John Wallace, already eighty years old. A highly renowned carver, Wallace was the only one with real experience in carving totem poles. Earlier, he'd been commissioned to carve two poles for the Department of the Interior in Washington, D.C., and in 1939 he had traveled to the World's Fair in San Francisco to demonstrate carving.

Workmen began collecting old poles from the unoccupied outlying villages, measuring, cataloging, and determining which were salvageable and which were too degraded to move. Meanwhile, Brown and his group of apprentices were organizing and beginning work at a carving shed in the Native village of Saxman, a few miles outside of Ketchikan, although later a carving shed was established at Mud Bight and most Tlingit poles were carved on site. Wallace and his men set up shop at Hydaburg on Prince of Wales Island; those completed poles were shipped to Mud Bight by boat. Their trainees had

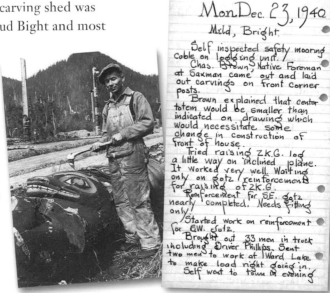

Mon. Dec. 23, 1940
Mild, Bright.

Self inspected safety mooring cable on leading unit. / Chas. Brown, Native Foreman at Saxman came out and laid out carvings on front corner posts.
Brown explained that center totem would be smaller than indicated on drawing which would necessitate some change in construction of front of house.
Tried raising Z.K.G. log a little way on inclined plane. It worked very well. Waiting only on go₁z / reinforcements for raising of Z.K.G.
Reinforcement for SE. go₁z nearly completed. Needs fitting only.
/Started work on reinforcement for GW. go₁z.
Brought out 33 men in truck including Driver Phillips. Sent two men to work at Ward Lake to make load right going in. Self went to town in evening.

RIGHT: *Tlingit carver Charles Brown at Saxman with pole to be copied and logbook entry noting a key visit by Brown to the site.*

virtually no experience with carving, having grown up in a time of incredible cultural upheaval. Pressured by non-Natives to give up their old ways and enter a wage-earning economy, the uncles, fathers, and grandfathers had largely ceased carving and no longer taught it to the young.

Forest Service architect Linn Forrest drew up plans for the grand Clan House that is today one of the most photographed stops in a walking tour of the park. He retained the classic lines of the old community houses that had once looked toward the water in every seaside village. The specifications included a spacious, single room with a central firepit, hewn cedar planks for walls and decks, and a gently sloping roof with a cleverly engineered smoke hole. Charles Brown would carve the four interior house posts that supported the roof beams, and although only the wealthiest clan painted their house front, this one would be painted with one of Brown's striking designs.

The CCC project wound down by June 1942, and with World War II siphoning money and laborers away from federal projects, the plan for a complete Mud Bight model village did not pan out. Instead, more attention was paid to the totems themselves and the focal point of the Clan House.

The outcome was a picturesque park with wide, green spaces at the edge of a dense forest. Pathways lined with fireweed and

Raising Front Totem Pole, P.I.V.C.H. Feb. 10, 1941.

Sat. Feb. 8, 1941
Summer Weather,
Stayed on wannie an last night and this morning brought property list up to date and checked property. About noon went to Ketchikan with Prasil. Did personal errands and went home about 3:00 P.M.

Mon. Feb. 10, 1941.
Mild, N'ly breeze
Raised Front Totem Pole and put temporary braces to hold it in position. Spent morning lowering butt of pole into hole and making final adjustments of tackle. About 1:30 started raising pole. It was raised and adjusted into place and plumbed without difficulty because of adaquate tackle. Working on Equipment Float Tower Line 3 2

Above: *Logbook entry and photo documenting the raising of the Clan House entrance pole.*

extraordinary totem poles stud the grounds as visitors approach the sea. The inviting Clan House faces the steel-gray waters, as it would have in a traditional village.

Mud Bight was renamed Totem Bight in 1946, and a few poles were raised as late as 1947. Visitors to Southeast during the post-war years were greeted with a half-dozen new totem parks and many individual poles resurrected in the cities. In all, forty-eight old poles were restored and another fifty-four, too far gone to save, were copied, wrote author Edward L. Keithahn in *Monuments in Cedar*. Another nineteen poles "existed only in memory," he wrote, and were newly carved. In addition to the Clan House at Totem Bight, two other community houses had been duplicated—one at New Kasaan, on Prince of Wales Island, and another at Shakes Island near Wrangell. Some 250 Natives had worked on totem restoration projects throughout the region.

When Alaska finally achieved statehood in 1959, Totem Bight was transferred from federal to state jurisdiction. In 1970, it was added to the National Register of Historic Places.

Over the years, uncounted visitors have marveled at the totems and the stories they depict, stories much older than the wood itself. More recently, Tlingit and Haida master carvers—not yet born in the CCC days—have been commissioned to repair or copy poles that were made for the park in the 1930s and '40s. As the founders had hoped, Totem Bight continues to offer a window into cultural history and provided a way, as tradition dictates, "for the uncles to teach the nephews."

ABOVE: *Framing the roof of the Clan House.*

Interpreting the Silent Storytellers

With these totem-posts and memorial poles of the dead, a view of the village has been compared to a harbour with its masts seen from a distance, or a pine forest after a great fire.

—Anthropologist Edward B. Tylor, 1899

In 1774, Spain was nervous about Russian activity in Alaska, and Captain Juan Perez was sent to investigate Spanish interests in "Nueva Galicia," as they called the Pacific Northwest. Along the beachfront villages of Prince of Wales Island, the sailors beheld enormous trees, stripped of their bark and carved with fantastic, wide-eyed creatures staring through the mist. Like others, the sailors mistakenly believed the poles were intended to frighten intruders. However, outsiders would not know their true purpose—their multiple purposes- -for many years to come.

Alaska's coastal Indians place great emphasis on personal humility, privacy, and respect for the oral histories, songs, and legends of other clans. Probing questions from foreigners often were met with a polite shrug or went unanswered. However, as friendship and trust developed, tribal authorities revealed more about their unwritten histories and traditions. By the late 1800s, some ancient stories, legends, and songs were recorded in print for the first time.

At the same time, some Christian missionaries were preaching that certain traditions, like carving, were spiritually harmful, and demanded that converts cease their centuries-old practices. An ancestor of contemporary carver Lee Wallace was among those who stopped carving. Wallace recognizes the chilling effect that the new religion had on the old ways, but says his grandfather came full circle. John Wallace, the Haida head carver for Totem Bight, was a church layman whose first language was Haida. Reading the Scriptures in English was something of a hindrance, Lee Wallace said, adding, "A lot of the time things are taken out of context, and I think for him it was, 'Here it is in black and white. I shouldn't be worshipping these images.' And here were these images he'd been carving his whole life." As John Wallace grew in his faith and understanding of Bible teachings, he reconciled beliefs with his skills in carving, knowing that he was not practicing idol worship. His son and grandson, both churchmen, also learned to carve.

11

WHAT WAS THE REAL MEANING?

Totem poles were and are an extension of the Tlingit, Haida, and Tsimshian cultures. Historically, the people carved to convey a message, as they lacked a written language. Some messages spoke of ownership; others helped remember a myth or story. Still others honored a person or event, or marked a grave. While not all three groups had all types of totem poles, various forms included:

House Frontal Poles – proclaiming matrilineal clan presence or ownership, these displayed the lineage of the house owner. Traditionally, these poles stood at or near the entrance of a clan or community house along the beach (see Pole 4 on page 29).

House Posts – interior upright carvings supporting the clan house roof, they usually told stories of the family crest.

Heraldic (Story or Legend) – figures serving as visual aids to retell a myth or share oral history. These poles started showing up in the nineteenth century as a basis for publicly displaying the ownership of important stories that deal with the respected ancestors. Pole on the Point (Pole 5 on page 33) is an original heraldic pole carved by Charles Brown.

Memorial – raised by the person selected to succeed as the head of the clan house. Memorial poles validated and transferred the status and titles of the deceased to his successor, who would place the pole in front of his house. Memorial poles may also honor a friend, remember a good deed or a great event. Totem Bight's Halibut Pole is a replica of a pole made to honor the Halibut House, which was located in Tuxekan on the north-west coast of Prince of Wales Island. The village is no longer occupied.

Mortuary or Grave Marker – while both marked a resting place, the former actually contained the remains or cremains of high-ranking clan members, which were placed in the back of the pole or in a box that was part of the pole. Totem Bight's Eagle Grave Marker (see Pole 2 on page 25) is an example of the latter type of pole, which was placed at a burial site.

Shame or Ridicule – calling attention to an unpaid debt, obligation, or a shameful act, such as the Seward Pole at Saxman Totem Park outside Ketchikan. In the late 1800s, visiting Secretary of State William H. Seward received gifts but did not reciprocate. Consequently, his image was carved atop a shame pole at Tongass Village. Traditionally, such a pole was removed after a debt was paid. There are no examples at Totem Bight, however a replica made during the CCC days stands at Saxman.

WHAT ARE THE FIGURES?

The images are intended to quicken the memory of the storyteller or viewer. The untrained eye sometimes needs help to make out distinct figures, as the carver may have entwined limbs, fins, beaks, human bodies, and spirit faces. In some instances, the viewer may see who's who in the figures, but still can't be certain of the pole's purpose without knowing the carver's intent. Even so, certain figures are usually easy to "read":

Bear: Watch for rounded ears, wide nostrils, and either a closed mouth or open jaws revealing teeth. Sometimes his tongue is hanging out.

Raven: His straight, black beak may be carved flat against the body or extended from the pole. Wings are often closed. He may have something in his mouth or grasped in his feet. Other birds at Totem Bight, such as the cormorant, are depicted similarly.

Thunderbird: Widespread wings, strongly curved yellow beak, and yellow legs. Curled "ears" or appendages extend past the top of its head.

Eagle: Like Thunderbird, his beak is yellow with a downward curved point; wings are usually spread slightly or against the body, but not always. The Eagle figure on the "Pole on the Point" has outstretched wings.

Devilfish or Octopus: Tentacles and suckers will be easy to spot.

Killer Whale: Also known as Blackfish, he has a strong dorsal fin and is often carved with an exposed row of menacing teeth.

Beaver: Watch for classic bucked teeth and cross-hatched tail. A figure may also have a stick in its mouth.

CARVING SHAPES

Balanced figures with symmetrical left and right sides are a hallmark of traditional Tlingit, Haida, and Tsimshian totems. Animals, birds, fish, and humans alike are carved with black, wide-open eyes in the shape of a rounded-edge rectangle. Around it another line finishes the ovoid eye shape. Slightly arched, thick black eyebrows are painted above each eye. Ovals meet at points and free-flowing curves in U and S shapes introduce graceful movement to the wood across cheeks, chin, or torso.

Bird figures are carved with ears atop their heads, like a bear's. Stylized feathers are cut into the wood. Raven's beak may tilt downward, flat against the bird's body or, at the top of a pole, protrude over an entwined stack of figures. Thunderbird's widespread wings are usually an attachment, while Eagle's, commonly closer to his body, are usually carved from the same tree trunk. The eagles at Totem Bight are exceptions, with wings that were carved from a separate piece. For both Eagle and Thunderbird, their beaks are thick and curved at the tip.

Traditional Tlingit poles may be carved the length of the tree, or not. Occasionally, a pole was designed with a single figure on top; below it, the tree remained uncarved. The long expanse of untouched wood might reference a physical position, such as with Thunderbird or Kadjuk, each of whom dwells in a high place, or it might indicate the prestigious position of that top figure, such as an honored chief or clan crest. Some Haida traditional poles included the carver's clan (Eagle or Raven) and crest images as well as his wife's clan, as demonstrated in the Master Carver Pole (No. 8) carved by John Wallace.

Because wild creatures might appear as humans at will, some were carved with a human face, blending the human flesh and animal spirit. Morphing between the animal and human worlds was routinely found in stories and legends, and story poles will depict that half-world. As anthropologist Keithahn wrote in his 1945 book, *Monuments in Cedar*, "Raven may be shown in human form but with a raven's wings, or with a human body and a raven's head. A whale might have a human face but will have in addition, a blowhole in the forehead. Dogfish sometimes are shown with human faces but with gill slit symbols in the cheeks. A squid or devilfish might appear as a human being but with tentacle suckers as eyebrows."

PAINT COLORS

Historically, Tlingit, Haida, and Tsimshian carvers used natural materials to create traditional paints in black, red, and brilliant blue-green. One anthropologist referred to the base as "a type of fish-egg tempera," in which the artist combined mineral pigment, fresh salmon eggs, and saliva. Red was created from cinnabar, hematite scrapings, iron oxide, or from the red pumice pebbles that floated ashore; black came from graphite and carbon; and the rich blue-green, used as a tertiary accent color, was made from copper oxide. Modern craftsmen have the advantage of mixing modern commercial paint to closely match traditional colors, while recognizing its drawbacks.

"It's pretty hard to come up with the exact duplication of the same color paint that was used long ago," said Nathan Jackson. Yellow, now seen on beaks and legs of certain birds, was not a traditional color, he said. It began appearing on carvings after contact with non-Natives.

"Yellow paint came along with boats," he said. "A lot of fishing boats, especially, started painting their booms or portions of their boats yellow." The bright color appealed to craftsmen, who began including it in the typical pallet for totem poles, and today it is commonplace.

TOOLS

In ancient times, carvers made their own tools using stone, bone, and flint attached to wooden handles with rawhide. With the availability of iron, craftsmen could create finer lines and smoother surfaces.

Today's traditional carvers often make their own tools, which include the adz and various knives, chisels, and gougers. Tlingit master carver Nathan Jackson, demonstrating his craft for visitors to Ketchikan, explains the uses of his favorite tools—both handmade and commercially made—their wooden handles dark and smooth from years of use. And yet, Jackson jokes with his audience, he's not above firing up a chainsaw for removing large sections of unwanted wood in the early, roughing-out stage.

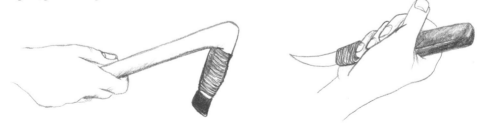

MAINTENANCE

The challenge for park groundskeepers is the maintainance of an all-wood outdoor museum set in a rainforest. Moisture, mold, insects, rot, and encroaching moss all add to a speedy decaying process. And battling the elements is an expensive effort. Over the years, various park improvement projects have kept the Clan House in condition, while other dollars funded replacements for a few poles. By the early twenty-first century, however, some poles were in a desperate state. Moss and vegetation had grown on the surfaces, and no paint had been added since the 1950s. With Capital Improvement Project funding from the state, workers removed the overgrowth and washed the poles, then applied a borate solution followed by a water repellent. The work continues. The same elements that for centuries destroyed poles in the wilderness are equally effective in the tamer setting of a park.

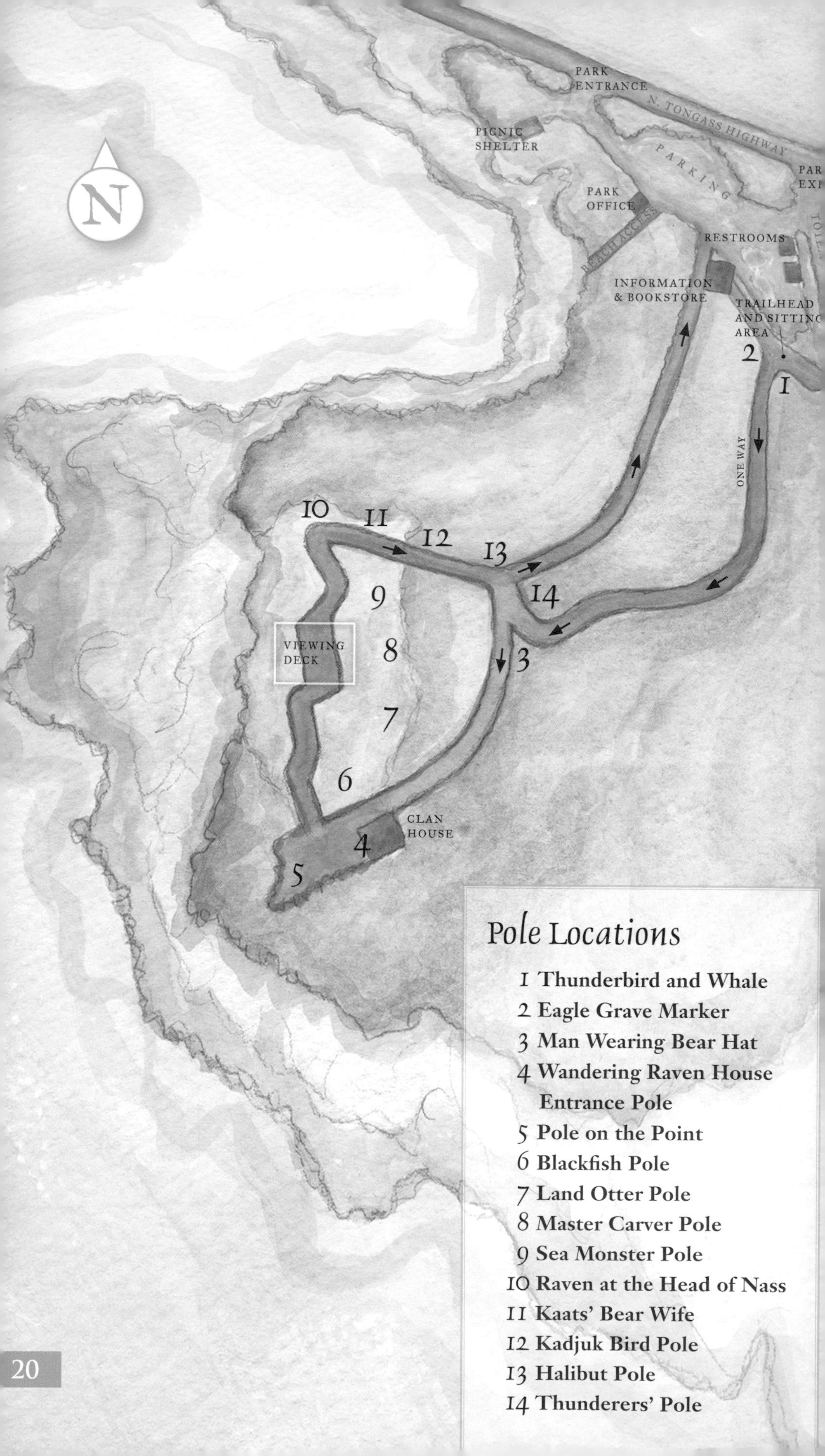

Map labels:

PARK ENTRANCE

N. TONGASS HIGHWAY

PICNIC SHELTER

PARKING

PAR EX

PARK OFFICE

RESTROOMS

BEACH ACCESS

INFORMATION & BOOKSTORE

TRAILHEAD AND SITTING AREA

TOL

ONE WAY

VIEWING DECK

CLAN HOUSE

N

Pole Locations

1 Thunderbird and Whale
2 Eagle Grave Marker
3 Man Wearing Bear Hat
4 Wandering Raven House
   Entrance Pole
5 Pole on the Point
6 Blackfish Pole
7 Land Otter Pole
8 Master Carver Pole
9 Sea Monster Pole
10 Raven at the Head of Nass
11 Kaats' Bear Wife
12 Kadjuk Bird Pole
13 Halibut Pole
14 Thunderers' Pole

The Totem Poles and Clan House

*The time is not far distant when these monuments will be considered
a resource as important to Southeastern Alaska and coastal British
Columbia as the pyramids are to Egypt or the ruins of ancient Rome to
modern Italy. The significant fact is simply that no other place in the
whole world has totem poles; people will come from far and wide to
see them . . . as long as they remain.*

– Edward L. Keithahn, *Monuments in Cedar*, 1945

Although no totems from pre-1800 survive, the ancient carvers
continue to teach through the oldest poles and their replicas. Many
Totem Bight poles are copies of originals carved long ago by skilled,
but unnamed men who knew their work would not last even two
generations in the rigors of the rainforest climate. In rare cases, a
wealthy man might commission a replica of a favored pole; however,
most simply fell to the ground, only to reenter the continuing cycle
of life from death.

In most creative forms, a copy might be viewed as an object of
lesser value than the original. In totem carving, however, the copy
may be even more meaningful, as contemporary craftsmen echo
the work of their ancestors.

At Totem Bight, Tlingit lead carver Charles Brown, of the
Nexadi clan, worked on many individual poles as well as on the
Clan House posts, and he designed the painting on the Clan House
front, that of a stylized raven with each eye elaborated into a face.
Haida master carver John Wallace, an Eagle born in Klinkwan, also
designed, labored and supervised carving on other poles. Typically,
a lead carver would transfer his design from paper onto the wood.
A team of younger carvers would rough out the design, and often
the master would make the finishing touches himself.

A walk into the historic park begins at the trailhead, where the
pavement meets the forest. There, visitors view the first of
fourteen historic totems.

THUNDERBIRD AND WHALE

The original Thunderbird and Whale mortuary pole once stood in the old village of Klinkwan on Prince of Wales Island. Haida master carver John Wallace made a copy in the late 1930s for Mud Bight. His carving stood until 1990, when Tlingit master carver Nathan Jackson was commissioned to create this replica of the great mythological bird holding a whale in its talons.

Writing in *Haida Monumental Art*, author George F. MacDonald described the attributes of the legendary creature: "[Thunderbird] lived in the mountains and came down to prey on whales. . . . Its wings represent the thundercloud and the flapping of its wings sounds like peals of thunder. The thunderbird killed whales with lightening, which it hurled from its mouth."

Viola E. Garfield and Linn A. Forrest wrote about the predator-and-prey relationship of Thunderbird and Whale in their 1948 book about the totem poles of Southeast Alaska, titled *The Wolf and the Raven*. "It is said that whale bones may be found on the tops of many mountains," they wrote, "where they have been carried in ages past."

Various versions of the Thunderbird story exist all along the Pacific Coast, crossing tribal lines from Alaska to Oregon. Other stories say Thunderbird's eyes were the source of lightening flashes and that its beating wings shook the very earth. Some scholars believe the legends are so similar because they're rooted in scientific truth— based on a seismic event dating from 1700, when a massive earthquake rocked the Northwest Coast.

EAGLE GRAVE MARKER

A unique Haida pole that draws elements from all three Southeast Alaska cultures also stands near the trail entrance. The original, found in the old village of Howkan, measured five and a half feet tall and more than four feet at its thickest. Old photographs depict a squat, commanding figure with a wide head. Originally the eagle marker was painted black with yellow beak and feet, and blue around its eyes. It had been adorned with copper plates and abalone shells, valuable items equated with the wealth of individuals who owned them. The marker was badly weathered when it was removed in 1941, silver-gray and stripped of its adornment. Although the present totem pole is based on that original, its dimensions and overall design differ.

In making his copy, master carver John Wallace made one deliberate, uncommon change: the addition of a Chilkat blanket across the eagle's breast and wings. In that portion of the carving, Wallace symbolically represented the mountain with a face, along with clouds and homes of creatures living in the mountains. Although today Chilkat blankets are viewed as a Tlingit art form, the weavings actually originated with the Tsimshian people. The Chilkat, from the northernmost part of the Southeast Panhandle, paid for the right to weave them, and eventually they became an important trade item.

According to authors Garfield and Forrest, Tlingit and Haida grave markers may be distinguished by the size of the tree. Extremely thick red cedar trees could be found in Haida lands, in the southern part of Alaska's Prince of Wales Island and further south in the Haida Gwaii region (Queen Charlotte Islands) of Canada. Consequently, shorter single figures carved from massive tree trunks suggest Haida heritage, whereas tall, thinner grave markers with a single crest figure on top are more likely Tlingit.

25

MAN WEARING BEAR HAT

This Tlingit pole is another example of a grave marker, found on Cat Island and copied by Charles Brown in the late 1930s. Fewer than sixty years later, Brown's copy had been so compromised by the weather that a replacement was necessary. Brown's second cousin, master carver Israel Shotridge, was commissioned to carve this replica in 1995.

The seated human figure gazes forward peacefully, his hands and feet in a non-threatening pose. Painted whale figures adorn the carved hat's brim beneath the bear's head grinning from the top. "Such a hat was worn at a potlatch or other important occasion, during which the stories it symbolizes were told or dramatized," wrote Garfield and Forrest in *The Wolf and the Raven*. The bear's mouth is carved with its teeth bared, wrote the authors, "as a reminder that the Bear people are proud and will attack their enemies."

The earlier copy made by Charles Brown was placed in storage until it can be further protected or restored.

WANDERING RAVEN
HOUSE ENTRANCE POLE

This original house-frontal pole was designed by Charles Brown, and the master carver also directed the carving. Visitors may pass through it, or a side entrance, to enter the Clan House. Brown also designed the vast painting across the house front of a stylized Raven. Likewise, he designed the Watchmen figures that flank the Entrance Pole, each dressed in anticipation of a potlatch.

Brown chose the Tlingit creation story of Raven and the Box of Daylight to top his design for the Entrance Pole, a massive column attached to the Clan House. Below Raven's box are the figures of a mink and a frog. And further downward, a standing man represents a legendary carver, Natsihline, who is clutching Killer Whale, also known as Blackfish. Natsihline is credited with bringing Killer Whale to life by carving him. See Pole 6, the Blackfish Pole, which illustrates the full story.

Further downward are other characters in the story of Raven bringing daylight to the people. The winged creature with the curved beak is the powerful chief, Raven at the Head of Nass—also featured in Pole 10—and just above the entrance oval, the female figure with the labret in her lower lip is Raven's mother.

Clan House *and* House Posts

In a traditional village, many people shared quarters in one Clan House with a central fire pit and smoke hole in the roof above it. Depending on status, they lived on different levels of the decked great room. Chiefs and their families rightfully enjoyed more privacy at the rear of the house behind a painted screen. Other important families occupied the more desirable spaces near the chief's family, with woven mats, boxes, or screens dividing their living areas. The poorest families and slaves were relegated to living toward the front of the house, nearer the door. Slaves kept the fire going for cooking and warmth, and performed other household chores.

The Totem Bight Clan House was designed by Linn Forrest based on a model of an early nineteenth-century Haida house that would have housed thirty to fifty people. Visitors may imagine walls hung with skins, blankets, clothing, and weapons. Bedding made of thick furs would have been laid atop woven cedar-bark mats and other skins. By day, the skins would have been rolled up and stored, with other housewares and important belongings, beneath removable planks in the floor. The

room was warmed by a central wood fire, and the air was filled with the scent of cooking and the murmurs of those living and working in the communal house.

In the typical Clan House, four house posts, sometimes carved with the same legend, supported the two massive roof beams. These illustrate the legend of Duk-toothl, or "Black Skin," the Tlingit strong man of the Raven moiety, always carved in the act of showing his strength by tearing a sea lion in half. In most carvings, he's wearing a headdress made of braided sea lion intestines. However, in these Charles Brown designs, he wears the white weasel-skin hat of his clansmen, reserved for those of high honor.

Today, Alaska Natives gather at the Totem Bight Clan House for community celebrations and recognize its significance in teaching others about how their ancestors once lived. Look for a black handprint on the back of one House Post, signifying the blessing of the elders when the Clan House was rededicated in 1991.

POLE ON THE POINT

This impressive heraldic pole is an original, designed and carved by Charles Brown and a team of apprentices. Standing sixty-eight feet tall, the pole is topped by a shaman in ceremonial garb, headdress, and fringed leather apron. The figures below him illustrate several adventures, among them, the story of the Chief's Nephew Who Fed Eagles, and below it, the story of a woman with a frog husband and children.

A version of The Woman Who Married the Frog was recorded in 1904, when the mother of Chief Katishan of Wrangell related it to ethnographer John R. Swanton. The story concerned a girl who became lost in the woods, where she met a man who was really a frog. They married and had two frog children. The girl's family searched for her without success. After a long time, the girl sent her frog children back to see their grandparents. The first time, the little frogs were put out of the house; the second time, they were followed when they hopped back to the lake. After much consideration, the girl's father enlisted the villagers to help drain the lake. They spied the girl, covered with frogs except for her face, pulled her out, and carried her home. The frogs followed and filled the house. After the people began killing the frogs with human bones, they went away. The storyteller ended her story this way: "Afterward the girl remained with her father, and the frogs did not bother her any more."

Nearer to the bottom of the Pole on the Point, Brown carved one of many stories concerning Raven, whose exploits as "the trickster" are legendary. In this particular tale, he is deceiving Cormorant, Halibut, and Grizzly Bear to the point of death.

See page 54 to read the story of Raven, Bear, and Cormorant as it was retold in 1948.

BLACKFISH POLE

CCC records indicate that this Blackfish Pole is a copy of an original Tlingit pole found on Tongass Island, in front of a clan house known as Forested Island House. It illustrates the legend of Blackfish (Killer Whale) and Natsihline, who was an accomplished sea lion hunter and carver who created Blackfish.

Toward the top of the pole, a special crest shows Blackfish's dorsal fin extending from Raven. Each tiny face represents a blowhole. Below the crest, Natsihline is holding Blackfish by the tail. In the story, Natsihline's efforts to prove himself a good hunter resulted in jealousy among his brothers-in-law, except for the youngest among them. During a sea lion hunt, they left Natsihline to die on an island. There he was drawn into the Sea Lion House, where he helped the Chief's injured son by removing a spear tip from his side. Natsihline was rewarded with more skills and returned to his wife. Natsihline planned revenge against his betrayers, carving a Blackfish of yellow cedar, which came alive when he put it in the water. He sent the Blackfish to attack the canoe of his brothers-in-law and drown the eldest men, but saved the youngest.

On the Blackfish Pole, the human figure toward the bottom represents the evil brothers-in-law. As for the "rest of the story," after the deaths of his brothers-in-law, Natsihline instructed Blackfish to help the people, not harm them. Occasionally they would find a freshly killed halibut or seal on their beach. The people took Killer Whale as their crest, and some reported seeing Natsihline at sea, riding the backs of two Blackfish.

LAND OTTER POLE

Haida master carver John Wallace is credited with designing and performing most of the carving on the original heraldic pole, named "Man Captured by Land Otters" when it was raised in 1947, a year before Wallace's death at age ninety. After five decades, in 1996, Tlingit master carver Nathan Jackson was commissioned to carve a similar pole, which is standing today.

At the top of the pole is a human wearing a dogskin headdress and holding an otter's tail in one hand. In the other is the magical carved club that he used to kill the otter after outwitting it. In Tlingit legend, the Land Otter People, or Kushtakas, were greatly feared because they could shape-shift into human or otter form. Often they were menacing, capturing and drowning humans. In this pole, the lower human figures represent drowned men who have been taken captive to the cave home of the land otters, where they will be transformed into otter beings. In that state, they will entice other humans to join them.

According to Jackson, the story associated with the original pole came from the village of Sukkwan, which in the Tlingit language means "strawberry land." There, both Tlingit and Haida people coexisted and intermarried, so it would have been permissible for a Wallace, a Haida man, to carve a Tlingit story.

However, after further research, Jackson expressed doubts about who carved it. "That pole was supposed to have been done by John Wallace," he said. "In looking at the stylization and the handling of figures, and even if he were to supervise that particular project and have some-body else do it, it didn't represent anything that John Wallace has done in times past. . . . The original copy didn't even compare in that particular pole. I did a little research, and I kind of goofed a little bit because I started with the idea of copying that other one. Then I started doing research, and I realized that 'Hey, I'm not doing the right thing.'"

So while the story figures are the same, Jackson's version is not a replica of the earlier pole. The octopus (or devilfish) carving at the base especially differs from the first pole.

MASTER CARVER POLE

Haida master carver John Wallace designed, carved, and supervised other carvers to retell the story of Master Carver, or Master Carpenter, who taught the Haida people how to carve long ago. This is an original Haida pole designed for the Mud Bight Project, raised in June 1941.

At the top, Wallace began by identifying himself as an Eagle, and added two Eagle crests, Beaver and Bullhead. Following Haida custom, Wallace next included his wife's Raven crest followed by clan crests of Bear, Blackfish and, at the base, Hoot Owl. The human figure above Hoot Owl is Master Carver himself, wearing a necklace of ten faces, representing ten lessons that Master Carver taught the Haida. In other carvings of Master Carver, the faces appear on his fingernails, but Wallace's design didn't allow room for detail that small.

Wallace included two shieldlike shapes below Bear. They represent hammered copper objects that symbolized great wealth, called Coppers or *tinnehs*, which were used as barter in coastal society. Coppers often were named for or by the chiefs who owned them, and they gained value with age and provenance as they changed hands. As a show of his power and wealth, a potlatch host might break a Copper into pieces, the modern equivalent of burning money.

SEA MONSTER POLE

In the late 1930s, John Wallace carved this pole, which resembles an earlier original that once stood in the now-uninhabited Haida village of Klinkwan, on Prince of Wales Island.

A village watchman peers out from about thirty-five feet high, and below him are two Eagle clan crests and faces that represent the mountains and clouds, where eagles dwell. The rest of the pole, however, embodies figures from the undersea world: Blackfish holding a seal, a legendary sea monster, and an octopus (devilfish) carved in the act of devouring a man. Keithahn wrote about the mythical sea monster in *Monuments in Cedar*, published in 1945. "Next to Raven, the most popular subject for totem pole art was the Gonakadet," he wrote. "Known also to the Haidas as 'Wasgo,' this monster is generally depicted as an aquatic wolf with some aspects of the Killer Whale. One story about it relates that it had a head like a 'house,' but whether this referred to shape or to its size is no longer known."

RAVEN AT THE HEAD OF NASS

Under the direction of Charles Brown, a team of CCC carvers copied an original Tlingit pole found on Tongass Island. The top figure is a chief wearing a spruce root hat; at the bottom is Raven at the Head of Nass, a powerful chief and Raven's grandfather. The human above him represents the ancestors of the Raven clan. The classic story also is illustrated on the Clan House Entrance Pole (Pole 4).

In one of the most foundational stories of Tlingit legend, Raven transforms himself into a hemlock needle in a cup of water. When the daughter of Raven at the Head of Nass drinks the water, she becomes pregnant. Her baby, Raven, is a demanding creature who cries until his grandfather, Raven at the Head of Nass, relents and lets Raven have the boxes in grandfather's house. Raven opens them and releases the moon and the stars, then cries and cries until Raven at the Head of Nass at last gives him the box of daylight.

To read Chief Katishan's fuller version of the story, see page 52.

KAATS' BEAR WIFE

The original Tlingit pole was located on Tongass Island, and Charles Brown made the first copy for the Mud Bight project. A she-bear peers down from the top of an otherwise uncarved pole that's painted with bear tracks. Almost fifty years later, Tlingit carver Israel Shotridge was commissioned to carve a replica of the bear, when he was still early in his career. Today he's considered a master carver, but in 1985, this was his first commissioned work, and a pole that held family ties.

"A lot of those totem poles out there are carved by my mother's cousin, a gentleman named Charlie Brown," Shotridge said. "I didn't know him, but I got to meet relatives later on. What's funny about replicating totem poles that Charlie Brown replicated back in the 1930s is that you kind of get to know him somewhat through his art."

The story of Kaats (pronounced "kotz") has many versions, one of which tells of a grizzly bear hunter whose dogs chased a boar; meanwhile, a female bear took him into her cave and married him. When he died at the hands of his bear children, his bear wife withdrew to the hills and sang a beautiful, mournful song. There are elements of shape-shifting in this story when bear appears in human form to the witness. In *The Wolf and the Raven*, authors Garfield and Forrest note, "Since that time the dirge has been sung by the descendants of Kaats . . ."

A more complete story of Kaats and His Bear Wife can be found on page 57.

KADJUK BIRD POLE

Cat Island, off of southwestern Annette Island, was the home of the original Tlingit pole on which this totem pole was patterned. Peering down from fifty-five feet above is the figure of Kadjuk, a mythological bird and the crest of the Kadjuk people of the Raven clan.

Anthropologist Edward L. Keithahn suggested that the golden eagle, rare in these parts, was perhaps the inspiration for the Kadjuk legend. "As the fable goes, this bird amuses itself by dropping stones on unsuspecting ground hogs," Keithahn wrote. "If one is lucky enough to acquire one of these stones, his prosperity is assured for all time."

The great expanse of undecorated pole, Keithahn suggested, symbolized his lofty caste as well as his habitat.

Below Kadjuk is Raven, who forms a headdress for his wife, Fog Woman. An important figure in Tlingit legend, Fog Woman created the first salmon, which faithfully return every year to feed the people. She is carved holding two salmon; below her are two faces representing Raven's slaves.

At the turn of the twentieth century, the house chief of the Kadjuks was Chief George Johnson, a Tongass Raven whose Native name was *Yash-noosh*. Chief Johnson's Pole, nearly identical to this one, was raised in 1901 in front of the chief's home at the mouth of Ketchikan Creek. Still standing when all surrounding old structures were razed, the pole was a Ketchikan landmark until 1982. Seven years later, amid great celebration, Israel Shotridge's replica pole was raised at the Tongass Historical Museum and Public Library. The original Chief Johnson Pole is now part of the Totem Heritage Center collection in Ketchikan.

See page 59 for Fog Woman's story.

HALIBUT POLE

The original Halibut Pole once stood in Tuxekan, a Tlingit village on Prince of Wales Island, where the pole honored the Halibut House people of the Nexadi clan. During the 1930s, when CCC workers were cataloging and collecting the old poles, it was removed and raised again at Mud Bight Village. In 1970, Tlingit carver Nathan Jackson created this replica of the single-figure bottomfish at the top of a plain post; the original is preserved at the Totem Heritage Center in Ketchikan.

A pole carved to honor another clan or person is often identifiable because there is little or no carving beneath the uppermost figure, a clan crest or carving representing an individual. The square pole was a style of carving characteristic of the people of Tuxekan.

THUNDERERS' POLE

A Thunder House pole from Tongass Island was copied for the CCC project, illustrating the Tlingit story of four brothers of the Wolf moiety, who were changed into Thunderers and lived among the Thunderbirds on the mountaintops.

A short pole in comparison to others in the park, it depicts a Thunderbird perched atop the head of a man, representing the four brothers.

In one story retold in 1904 by the mother of Wrangell Chief Katishan, the brothers are distressed when their sister disappears with a youth. The men hunt for their sister and find her stuck, a snail coiled around her, halfway up a cliff. They try to fashion wings of wood or bone to fly up to her, and finally succeed in freeing her. In the words of the storyteller, who shared the myth with anthropologist John R. Swanton: " . . . the four brothers now left their own village, because they said that their sister had disgraced them, and they became Thunders [sic]. When they move their wings, you hear the thunder, and, when they wink, you see the lightning."

A Sampling of
Legends & Stories

Pole 4

WANDERING RAVEN

Raven and The Box of Daylight.
RETOLD BY WRANGELL CHIEF KATISHAN TO JOHN R. SWANTON, 1904.

At the beginning of things there was no daylight and the world lay in blackness. Then there lived in a house at the head of Nass River a being called Raven-at-the-Head-of-Nass (*Nâs-cA'kî-yêl*), the principal deity to whom the Tlingit formerly prayed but whom no one had seen; and in his house were all kinds of things including sun, moon, stars, and daylight. . . .
. . . First of all beings, *Nâs-cA'kî-yêl* created the Heron as a very tall and very wise man and after him the Raven, who was also a very good and very wise man at that time. Heron and Raven both became servants to *Nâs-cA'kî-yê*l, but he thought more of Raven and made him head man over the world. Then *Nâs-cA'kî-yêl* made some people.

All of the beings *Nâs-cA'kî-yêl* had created, however, existed in darkness, and this existence lasted for a long time, how long is unknown. But Raven felt very sorry for the few people in darkness and, at last, he said to himself, "If I were only the son of *Nâs-cA'kî-yêl*, I could do almost anything." So he studied what he should do and decided upon a plan. He made himself very small, turned himself into a hemlock needle, and floated upon the water that *Nâs-cA'kî-yêl's* daughter was about to drink. Then she swallowed it and soon after became pregnant.

After a while, the baby began to crawl about. His grandfather thought a great deal of him and let him play with everything in the house. Everything in the house was his. The Raven began crying for the moon, until finally they handed it to him and, quick as a wink, he let it go up into the sky. After he had obtained ev-erything else, he began to cry for the box in which daylight was stored. He cried, cried, cried for a very long time, until he looked as though he were getting very sick, and finally his grandfather said, "Bring my child here." So they handed Raven to his grandfather. Then his grandfather said to him, "My grandchild, I am giving you the last thing I have in the world." So he gave it to him.

Then Raven, who was already quite large, was walking down along the bank of Nass River until he heard the noise people were making as they fished along the shore for eulachon in the darkness. All the people in the world then lived at one place at the mouth of the Nass. They had already heard that *Nâs-cA'kî-yêl* had something called "daylight," which would some day come into the world, and they used to talk about it a great deal. They were afraid of it.

Then Raven shouted to the fishermen, "Why do you make so much noise? If you make so much noise, I will break daylight on you." Eight canoe loads of people were fishing there. But they answered, "You are not *Nâs-cA'kî-yêl*. How can you have the daylight?" and the noise continued. Then Raven opened the box a little and light shot over the world like lightning. At that, they made still more noise. So he opened the box completely and there was daylight everywhere.

THE CLAN HOUSE HOUSE POSTS

Duk-Toothl (or *Ka-Ha-Si*), from
Monuments in Cedar.
By EDWARD L. KEITHAHN, 1945.

In old *Taqdjik-an* (Tuxekan), the ancient seat of the Klawak people, dwelt Galwet, a chief of the Takwanedi or "Winter People." Every day he bathed in the sea for strength and his people bathed with him. In the cold, gray mornings he would rise, run down to the sea, and rush in, followed by his clan. Then they would whip each other with switches until their blood ran hot.
After that they would go to a certain tree where the Chief attempted to pull a branch out. Then they would go to another tree which the Chief tried to twist from top to bottom. He was testing his strength in preparation for an expedition against the sealions.

Galwet had a nephew and an heir who was a great disappointment to the entire village. He was weak and cowardly and would lie abed when all the others were bathing for strength. They called him *Duk-toothl* or "Black skin" because he never bathed and was blackened with soot from sleeping close to the fire. One day, however, his aunt took him in hand secretly, told him how he was disgracing the clan, that they would lose caste when he became chief. He promised her that he would make himself strong and worthy of the respect normally accorded a chief.

[Afterward, Black skin decided to bathe and prepare himself to join the others for a sealion hunt. One night as he bathed, he met Strength and was changed. He suffered the teasing of the others in the canoe on the way

53

to the hunt. On the island, his uncle, Galwet, was killed by a sealion, and Black-skin disembarked and walked straight up the cliff, seeking his uncle's killer.]

The small sealions in his way he killed simply by hitting them on the head with his fist or by stepping on them. He was looking only at the big bull that had killed his uncle, for he did not want it to get away. When he finally reached it he grasped it by the hind flukes and tore it in two.

After he had killed all the sealions he loaded the canoe with them. But before he could get into the boat, his companion shoved off, leaving him stranded.

[Black-skin was taken to live among the sealion people, whom he saw as humans. When he helped cure a wounded child, the sealion people gave him a box that could bring any kind of wind. Black-skin used the box to return home, where those that had been cruel to him were ashamed.]

They had thought that he would avenge himself on them, but he talked to them in a kindly manner saying, "So do not make fun of poor people again as you did when my uncle was alive."

After this day, Blackface was known no longer by his nickname but by his true name, *Ka-ha-si*.

Pole 5

POLE ON THE POINT

The story of *Raven, Bear, and Cormorant* is one of three stories that Charles Brown carved onto one pole. It is retold in *The Wolf and the Raven*. By Viola E. Garfield and Linn A. Forrest, 1948.

Raven was wandering around the country with Cormorant as his companion or slave. He met a pair of bears with whom he became very friendly. He suggested to the male bear that they go halibut fishing, taking Cormorant along to paddle, bail, and otherwise serve as his slave.

Raven caught many halibut, but Bear caught nothing. Bear asked Raven what kind of bait he was using. Raven mumbled something Bear did not understand and went on fishing. He again asked Raven what kind of bait he used, and Raven finally told him to cut a piece of meat off of himself if he wanted to catch halibut. Bear protested, but Raven told him his wife would be very angry if he came home without any halibut. Then he began to taunt Bear and call him a coward because he was afraid to cut a piece of meat from himself for bait. Raven wanted to kill Bear anyway because he did not want to share his catch with him. Finally Bear did as Raven directed and bled to death.

Raven then thought how he could prevent Cormorant from telling what had happened. He turned to Cormorant, who was paddling, and said excitedly, "Wait, wait, look this way! What is that in your mouth? Open it and hold still. It is on your tongue! Stick it out." The bewildered Cormorant opened his mouth and stuck out his tongue and Raven took hold of it and pulled it out. "Now talk," jeered Raven, but Cormorant could only mumble.

When Raven and Cormorant reached shore, the female bear asked about her husband. Raven said, "He got off beyond the point and will walk over. He will be here by nightfall." Cormorant tried to tell her what happened. Raven said, "He is trying to tell you that the fishing was very good."

Raven began to cook the halibut, and he thought how he could kill the female bear. He cut out the halibut stomachs and filled them with red hot rocks. When they were ready he called her and said, "People do not chew what I cook. Swallow it whole." She followed directions and soon was in great pain. Raven told Cormorant to bring her water to drink. Steam came from her mouth and she soon died. Raven then ordered Cormorant to go out and sit on the rocks offshore, and that is where cormorants are seen now. Raven ate all the halibut and bear meat himself.

Pole 7

LAND OTTER POLE

Man Captured by Land Otters is illustrated in this Haida pole by John Wallace. It is retold in *The Wolf and the Raven.*
By Viola E. Garfield and Linn A. Forrest, 1948.

One day a man and his family, who were Eagle clansmen, went to Cape Muzon to camp. He took his dog and went hunting in the canoe. A storm came up, and he capsized, but he and the dog were able to swim to shore.

When he reached the beach he quickly killed the dog and put the skin over his head to protect himself from the power of the land otters, whom all Haida dread. He walked along the beach and saw a cave in which two naked men were sitting. Their ears and heads looked like those of otters, but their bodies were still human, and he recognized them as men who had recently drowned.

The next day the man saw two people who looked like his brother and sister coming toward him. He listened carefully and knew from their speech that they were really land otters impersonating his relatives in order to capture him. He killed them with his carved club. Every day some of his relatives came pleading with him to go home with them, and every day he killed them because he knew they were really land otters. The dog skin gave him power to recognize them for what they were.

One day his sister and brother again approached him. He listened to their conversation and they talked correctly. To test them he asked his sister for tobacco, which she gave him. Then he knew that they were his relatives, for land otters have no tobacco. He went home with them, related all of his adventures, and carved the story to commemorate his escape.

Pole 8

MASTER CARVER POLE

Master Carver, or **Master Carpenter**, **retold in** *The Wolf and the Raven.* BY CARVER JOHN WALLACE, 1948.

Long ago the Haida did not know how to carve, and Master Carver came and taught them. When he came he wore a carved and painted headdress, and a blanket shirt woven of mountain-goat wool, richly ornamented with designs. His body was tattooed with crest figures. A halo of bright light shone around him, hence he is painted a light color instead of dark as an ordinary human being would have been painted. On his fingernails were human faces, each with a different design and expression. [Because the figure was not large enough to put faces on the nails, John Wallace carved the faces as a necklace for Master Carver.]

When Master Carver appeared to the Haida, he told them, "Tonight something will happen. Go to bed as usual and pay no attention to anything you may hear. Don't look

until you are sure that the sun is up." During the night the people heard chopping but they covered their heads and restrained their curiosity as he had instructed them. In the morning they saw that the corner posts of the house had been carved and the partition at the back of the house had been painted with animal and human figures. They went outside and there were three carved poles in front of the house, one in the center and one at either corner. The whole front of the house was covered with carved and painted figures. The people were amazed for these were the first carved and painted figures they had ever seen. They studied everything carefully and tried to copy what they saw.

Master Carver came again and instructed the men. Each day he pointed to one of the faces on his nails and explained the experience behind it. Thus, lesson by lesson, he taught the Haida the secrets of carving. He urged them to study and gave them directions for the different kinds of medicines and training necessary for successful work.

Pole 11

KAATS' BEAR WIFE

The story of *Kaats and His Bear Wife* belongs to the Kaats Hit people of the Taantakwaan Teikweidi, the Tongass Brown Bear clan. It appeared in the first edition of *The Wolf and the Raven* in 1948.

Long ago on Rudyerd Bay lived a family in which there were four boys. One day Kaats, the eldest, took his dogs and went into the woods to hunt grizzly bear. He traveled far up the mountain, his dogs running on ahead. Suddenly they came upon a den in which two grizzly bears lived. The dogs barked, and the old male bear came out. He grabbed the young man and threw him into the den. As Kaats fell, he involuntarily reached for something to save himself and touched the she-bear. Immediately she was changed [and appeared as a woman to Kaats]. She quickly dug a hole in the floor and hid him. When her husband had chased off the dogs he came in and asked where the man was. The she-bear answered, "You didn't throw any man in here, you only threw a mitten in." He searched but could find nothing. Angrily he left the den...

[When Kaats did not return, his three brothers prepared to

search for him. But they did not follow the preparation rituals strictly, except for the youngest brother. When he found Kaats, he was told to wait until spring, when the bears came out of their dens.]

 ...The family watched constantly for Kaats's return, and one day they saw him with his bear wife and cub children coming across the flats toward the village. They stopped, and the bear wife instructed her husband not to look at his human wife to try to speak to her. Then he went on into the village. Kaats and one of his fellow tribesmen hunted seal, which he took to his bear wife and cubs. When his luck was good he brought back two or three. Only then would the bear get some. When there was only one the cubs ate all of it, forgetting their mother...

 ...One day when Kaats was returning from seal hunting, his human wife hid behind one of the houses. As he came past she stepped out, and he could not help looking at her. His bear wife immediately knew what had happened. Later he landed in front of her camp as usual, and walked right up to her, though he knew that he had done something she had forbidden. She got up and said, "I told you not to look at that former wife of yours," and with that admonition gave him a gentle shove. She knew he could not prevent it and did not intend to punish him. However, the cubs sprang upon him and tore him to pieces before their mother could save him...

 After her husband's death the bear turned around they went up into the hill country. As she walked slowly up the mountain she sang a song of sorrow:

> *I wonder where my husband has gone.*
> *I wonder where my husband has gone.*
> *He left me.*
> *He left me.*

 As she went along, her husband's sealing partner heard her singing. He learned the song and went back to the village and told the people what had happened. Since that time the dirge has been sung by the descendants of Kaats, and the post was carved to commemorate his fate. They also took the name, Kaats House, by which they and their dwelling have since been known.

KADJUK BIRD POLE

Fog Woman
RETOLD BY ESTHER TAA'LYEI SHEA, OF THE TEIKWEDI TAANTAKWAAN
(BROWN BEAR, TONGASS TRIBE), 1994.

Long ago, Raven was fishing from his canoe with two human companions, but they only caught bullheads. As they turned to head home, a heavy fog closed them in and they did not know which way to go. Suddenly there appeared a woman sitting right in their canoe. She asked Raven for his spruce root hat, and as she held it, all the fog disappeared into it. The sun shone clearly and they were able to see their way home. Back in camp, they brought Fog Woman a basket of fresh water from the spring. She dipped her finger in it and told them to spill the water out toward the sea. When they did this, the whole stream was filled with swimming salmon, which they caught and brought back to camp. Fog Woman instructed them to build a smokehouse, and they went to work smoking and preserving the bounty of miraculous fish for winter storage.

Before too long, however, Raven became disenchanted with Fog Woman and he began to treat her with disrespect. When she realized he would not change his bad ways, she decided to leave him and his camp. As she walked toward the sea, Raven tried to hold her back, but she slipped through his grip like a foggy mist. As she disappeared, all the salmon followed her down into the water. Raven was very sad. Fog Woman took pity on him however, so she sent her daughter, Creek Woman, to the head of every stream of the land. It is Creek Woman who calls each year the salmon to return to the place of their birth and give abundance to the people.

A *Living* Heritage

Few Native men were carving in the early 1900s, yet a century later, the tradition is flourishing again. Awesome in size and beauty, monumental poles hold command in government properties, town squares, parks, museums, and in collections all over the world. And today's elder craftsmen are maintaining their cultural charge to instruct "the nephews," literally and figuratively, teaching younger carvers through apprenticeships, classes, and demonstrations.

Among today's masters, three have a special connection to Totem Bight: Nathan Jackson, Israel Shotridge, and Lee Wallace. Jackson and Shotridge have replicated or repaired about a third of the park's poles. Wallace is a descendant of CCC Haida carver John Wallace, and Shotridge is related to Tlingit carver Charles Brown.

Each man's work is recognizable for its individual style, and the strong influences of the ancestral carvers.

"It's too bad we didn't get to see or talk to any of these guys," Jackson once told a reporter, "because they were pretty good themselves. It'd be dandy to get a critique here or there."

NATHAN JACKSON
Yelch Yedi, **Salmon Clan of the Chilkoot Tlingit**

Jackson may be the most famous living Alaskan carver. Born in 1938, he learned the ways of his people—stories, songs, and how to fish—from his clan uncle and grandfather, Jack Davis. Formally trained at New Mexico's Institute of American Indian Arts, he began carving miniature totem poles as a young man during a lengthy hospitalization. Today Jackson's commissions—masks, bentwood boxes, house posts, and totems—are in great demand. Installations include the National Museum of the American Indian in Washington, D.C., the Burke Museum in Seattle, and the Alaska State Museum in Juneau, among many notable venues.

LEFT: *Stephen Jackson began carving at age four learning the tradition from his father, renowned Tlingit carver Nathan Jackson.*

Visitors to Ketchikan may find Jackson working in the carving shed of Saxman Totem Park, where he carves, teaches, and speaks to tourists.

Commenting on poor imitations of Tlingit, Haida, and Tsimshian carvings, Jackson spoke of a state program in which Native-made art is tagged with a silver hand logo, assuring buyers that their purchases are authentic.

"The Silver Hand Program makes a difference in Alaska," Jackson said. "There's a lot of fakers."

ISRAEL SHOTRIDGE
Kinstaádaál, **Bear Clan of the Tongass Tlingit**

Shotridge, born in 1951, is his tribe's designated Tribal Carver. Totem Bight carver Charles Brown was a first cousin of Shotridge's mother, the late Esther Shea.

"There's not that many that replicate totems," said Shotridge. "You have to do your research, and [my mother] helped me understand what the totem pole was about and what the story is, so when I'm carving the totem pole, I have a greater appreciation and a broader view of our culture."

Aside from numerous commissions for original works, Shotridge has replicated poles at Totem Bight, Klawock, Saxman, and downtown Ketchikan, including the famed Chief Johnson Totem Pole and Chief Kyan Pole.

"I got to know these artists," he said, "even though they're not with us. It's a funny thing."

In a circling-back, the U.S. Forest Service commissioned Shotridge to carve a totem pole commemorating the 1930s CCC carvers for display at the agency's "Hall of Tribal Nations" exhibit in Washington, D.C.

LEE WALLACE
Guugwaangs, Tlingit, Haida, and Tsimshian heritage

Born in 1953, Wallace is descended from a line of famous Haida carvers. His great-grandfather, Dwight Wallace (c. 1822-1913), skillfully carved the Old Witch Pole, now more than a century old, restored, and on display in the atrium of the State Office Building in Juneau. Lee's grandfather was John Wallace (1851-1948), who dedicated the last decade of his life working on poles for Totem Bight. And Lee's late father, William Wallace, was a fisherman and a skilled carver.

As for Lee Wallace, he is perhaps the best-known Haida carver of his generation, with commissioned works in museums and public places around the world. Ketchikan visitors may view his multi-totem work, Council of the Clans, on the grounds of Cape Fox Lodge. With his apprentice, Wallace carved two totems for the Nesbett Courthouse in Anchorage. And in 1996, his Wasgo totem was installed at the Eiteljorg Museum of American Indians and Western Art in Indianapolis.

In another circling-back story, Wallace tells of the pole his grandfather carved in the 1930s as a gift for the Prince of Wales cannery. The pole disappeared after the cannery closed, resurfacing years later, when it was restored and installed in Seattle's East Montlake Park. In 2007, the cannery, now a sport-fishing resort, commissioned Lee Wallace to carve two poles retelling his grandfather's "Story of North Island."

A year later, Wallace restored another of his grandfather's masterpieces, the famed "Story Master," or "Four Story Pole," which John Wallace carved as a CCC project in 1940. The pole stood at a Hydaburg cannery for twenty years before it was moved to Juneau's elementary school, and there it lived for another thirty years. Wallace was hired to restore the pole before it was moved yet again to a new home outside the Juneau-Douglas City Museum, where it has stood since 1994. In 2008, Wallace was invited back to Juneau to restore the seventy-year-old Four Story Pole for a second time.

While in Juneau, Wallace chanced to see the famed Old Witch Pole, which his great-grandfather had carved in about 1880, and was once more humbled by the skills of his long-dead ancestor.

"That was some fine carving," he said, "and to date I haven't carved anything like it."

Learn More

CONTEMPORARY READING

Clark, Ella E. *Indian Legends of the Pacific Northwest*. Berkeley: University of California Press, 2003. Originally published, 1958.

Dauenhauer, Nora Marks and Richard Dauenhauer. *Haa Shuka, Our Ancestors*. Seattle: University of Washington Press, 1987.

Emmons, George T., Jean Low, and Frederica de Laguna, ed. *The Tlingit Indians*. Seattle: University of Washington Press, 1991.

Garfield, Viola E. and Linn A. Forest. *The Wolf and the Raven: Totem Poles of Southeastern Alaska*. Revised edition. Seattle: University of Washington Press, 1961. Original hardcover, 1948.

Jonaitis, Aldona. "Totem Poles and the Indian New Deal," *The Canadian Journal of Native Studies*, IX:2, (1989):237-252.

Keithahn, Edward L. *Monuments in Cedar*. Second edition. Seattle: Superior Publishing Co., 1963. Originally published, 1945.

Knapp, Marilyn and Sue Thorsen. *Carved History: The Totem Poles and House Posts of Sitka National Historical Park*. Revised edition. Anchorage: Alaska Geographic Association, 2008. Originally published, 1980.

Langdon, Steve. *The Native People of Alaska*. 4th edition. Homer, Alaska: Wizard Works, 2002.

Lewis, James G. *The Forest Service and the Greatest Good: A Centennial History*. Durham, N.C.: Forest History Society, 2005.

Wright, Robin K. *Northern Haida Master Carvers*. Seattle: University of Washington Press, 2001.

VIDEO

Serrill, Ward, Esther Shea, and Priscilla Schulte. *"The Bear Stands Up," a biography of Tlingit tradition bearer Esther Shea*. Ketchikan: University of Alaska Southeast, 1994.

ARCHIVAL TEXTS

Dixon, Capt. George. *A Voyage Round the World, 1785-88*. London: George Goulding, 1789.

Dorsey, George A. "A Cruise Among Haida and Tlingit Villages About Dixon's Entrance," *Appleton's Popular Science Monthly*. United States: D. Appleton, 1898.

Frobese, F. E. *The Origin and Meaning of the Totem Poles in Southeastern Alaska*. Sitka: Alaska Printing Office, 1897.

Malaspina, Alejandro. *The Malaspina Expedition 1789-1794*. The Journal of the Voyage by Alejandro Malaspina, Vol. II. Andrew David, Felipe Fernandez-Armesto, Carlos Novi, and Glyndwr Williams, eds. London: Hakluyt Society, 2003. Originally published, 1885.

Shotridge, Louis. "House Posts and Screens and Their Heraldry," *The Museum Journal*. Philadelphia: The University Museum, 1913.

Swanton, John R. *Tlingit Myths and Texts*. Washington, D.C.: U.S. Bureau of American Ethnology, Bulletin 39, 1904.

U.S. Bureau of American Ethnology. *Social Condition, Beliefs, and Linguistic Relationship of the Tlingit Indians*. Washington, D.C.: U. S. Bureau of American Ethnology, Annual Report 26, 1904–1905.

Vancouver, Capt. George. *A Voyage of Discovery (1790-95)*. London: G. G. and J. Robinson, 1798.